The Fruits Of Favor And Increase

By

ANTHONY MONTOYA

The Fruits Of Favor And Increase

By

Anthony Montoya

Published By:

ABM Publications

A division of Andrew Bills Ministries Inc.

PO Box 6811, Orange, CA 92863

www.abmpublications.com

ISBN: 978-1-931820-45-5

DEDICATION

I would love to dedicate this book to my family & friends, who helped me through my walk of life. I would love to thank, David, Lupita, Nathaniel Sanchez & family, Pauli & Jack Taniguchi, My brothers Adrian Calderon and Robert Briseno for aiding me for shelter when I was living in my car. Also Prophet Mark, Sharon Sohmer, Mama McGee and Stevie. Prophetess Karen & Gilbert Bowser aiding me for shelter and food for several months. Prophetess Marie Santilliano for aiding me with intercession one night when I was in urgent need of a demonic attack, I was not supposed to be attending certain meetings where these spirits of warlocks and witches were even though they were apostles and prophets, I called Marie at midnight, I was being choked by a python spirit through a false prophet who astro projected out of his body and controlled another person to walk over to me and lay hands on me. She called it out within seconds and then rebuked me and corrected me. Prophetess Cynthia from Riverside California, Prophetess Cynthia from Glendale California. Prophetess Veronica from Rialto California, she called me one night while I was being attacked by the spirit of rejection & abandonment a dark heavy cloud, haven't spoke to her in three years and she called out of know where and broke the stronghold off me.

I would also like to thank, Prophetess Lily & Luis Avila, Sara, Denise, Prophet Brian & Claudia. Prophet Andre Hardin & Wife Pamela, Apostle Al Fornis for a major deliverance and breakthrough, Prophetess Deanne, Prophet Carlton LaGrange. Prophet Donnie from Louisiana who prophesied to me in detail and stated I had to wait 9 more months, and then I was removed from the burden of being homeless. Prophet Garret Lloyd, Prophet Michael Hodges & Family taking me through heavy healing and Deliverance. Prophet Hue Fortson taking me through heavy deliverance. Prophetess Stacy Yada, Apostle David Vizcara for aiding with money and material things. Prophet Alex & family, Prophetess Anita Morvac for her intercession, Prophetess Cindy from Upland California. Prophetess Young for her hospitality from Covina California. I would love to thank my brother Andrew from Corona California, Albert Garcia & family, Monique, Laura for aiding me food and money. Also I would love to thank Juan Valdez for shelter and food for several months. Prophet Evan walker for breaking a certain stronghold an affirming that it was over. My Parents Mary & Santiago for their tender loving care and hospitality.

TABLE OF CONTENTS

ANTHONY MONTOYA

FOREWORD

It is with much excitement and honor that I get the opportunity to acquaint you with my friend Anthony Montoya. In his unique style he reflects authentic leadership, tempered by a deep compassion for the lost.

In this age of religious phonies and spiritual apathy, Anthony does not compromise the unfailing word of God.

His passion and exuberance for God is infectious; Challenging Christians to draw closer to God and take the Bible serious. During a time I was seeking a speaker for my Ministry, God said to me "call Anthony". God used Anthony to confirm some important future Ministry events that He had already spoken to me about.

For the reasons above, and others that followed, I look forward to future Ministry with Anthony where his gifts will edify and be a blessing to the Body of Christ.

Lilly Avila – Rays of Glory Ministries, Inc.

ANTHONY MONTOYA

ACKNOWLEDGEMENT

In all the 19 years I have known Anthony Montoya, he has been very poised and consistent. He is a man I know who rightly divides the word of truth.

He carefully hears from the Holy Spirit and he speaks as the Spirit gives him the utterance. I highly recommend his work to any reader out there.

Lloyd Nsek

Author of "Christianity the End of Spiritual Confusion"

INTRODUCTION

Family which you are about to read has wandered through Christian beliefs and doctrine's, it states in the word to be careful and refrain from myths, fables & endless genealogies. Much speculations of purples talk, rather than stewardship, Yahweh's redemptive plan love & belief. You can assure yourself to be free from guilt, shame, unworthiness, false hope, rejections & abandonment. It gives precise specific understanding where is derives from. Family we all as a whole need to be very careful and refrain from the spirit of religion & influence. We must come to the end of self, die to self & lay down our own self will.

Most cases us as human beings live off of our own self-centeredness, also what has been falsely impregnated in our spirits, eggs that were thrown in by teachings, prophecies, impartations using reverse parapsychology influences. You may be wondering how, someone who has a big title, great name, the ministry involved in your circle or friendship using the gifts and talents in the name of God. Selling the birth & death of his resurrection, we need to ask the Holy Spirit to show us the motive and intentions of the heart of

others & to ask for the discernment of discerning
of spirits which the body lacks greatly.

Chapter 1

I am going to explain more about tithing and also the coming of Yeshua and where such mystical references accumulate misused doctrine. Hello Family, this significance and illustration is to point all the glory to Yahweh, Yeshua, and Holy Spirit. The Bible my beloved family speaks in many cases about Hospitality and taking care of those of your household first and relatives. The body of Christ has been mislead to forget about the poor or those in need & taking advantage of lost wounded souls. In Amos 5:10-12 There are those who hate the one who upholds justice in court and detest the one who tells the truth. [11] You levy a straw tax on the poor and impose a tax on their grain. Therefore, though you have built stone mansions, you will not live in them; though you have planted lush vineyards, you will not drink their wine. [12] For I know how many are your offenses and how great your sins.

The Amplified Bible references Amos 5:11, (Therefore because you tread upon the poor and take from him exaction's of wheat). Exaction – Dictionary reference extortion for usury (an excessive or harsh demand, esp. for money; extortion). I will get to this paraphrase of understanding about stealing and robbing those in need. There are only a few verses in the Bible which speak of going to hell. The Bible is speaking about the poor minded also, those who are in pain or emotional distress. Great titles lure away unstable souls to believe in what they practice preaching.

Most of us have not read the Bible and studied the word for ourselves; we have made our Pastors our idols. We have also given our hearts to our leaders to believe whatever they say instead of searching out the Scriptures for ourselves; also for the Holy Spirit to be our guide. Most Christians have encountered selfish intentions all for themselves and proclaim they have an insight of what they understand. Really, in many congregations, circles, ministries, or wherever family or acquaintances are involved, you won't give your hard working money to the brother or sister right next to you. You get all religious on them just like many fortresses, giving out a membership application for approval to what you think is needed and still never aid anyone.

Everyone wants to believe and think that pouring out your tithe in the offering basket to great leaders is going to make you prosper and have great wealth. There is nothing wrong with giving and honoring Yeshua and the working of His

Kingdom. Most leadership have not imparted to the children of Yahweh to understand Hospitality. What's wrong with giving your portion of money to those in need right next to you, that's considered the poor. Its not a popular practice in the body of Christ; the religious mentality belief has been planted into the church through their leaders manipulating their followers to believe that through their giving or them attending these conferences and meetings of teachings, they will receive an impartation of prosperity. They use this announcement as a marketing tactic for private gain. They will also announce come to this service or you will miss it, or come to this special conference and receive this prosperity impartation.

Romans 15:25-27 For the present, however, I am going to Jerusalem to bring aid (relief) for the saints (God's people there) [26] For it has been the good pleasure of Macedonia and Achaia to make some contribution for the poor among the saints of Jerusalem. [27] They were pleased to do it; and surely they are in debt to them, for if these Gentiles have come to share in their [the Jerusalem Jews'] spiritual blessings, then they ought also to be of service to them in material blessings. Wow, it states in the Bible to give to the poor and also in material wealth, as a body of

Christ most circles or ministries do not pass out money or support giving back in material wealth. It's all for themselves to build there great Kingdom and most of us are blind because you have no clue what Discerning of Spirits is. Saints, let me explain seed to you in some brief specific instructions, many of us have been manipulated by parapsychology influences to believe sowing your seed of money will do the job.

1 Corinthians 15: 33-38 says, Do not be so deceived *and* misled! Evil companionship (communion, associations) corrupt *and* deprave good manners *and* morals *and* character. [34] Awake [from your drunken stupor and return] to sober sense *and* your right minds, and sin no more. For some of you have not the knowledge of God [you are utterly and willfully and disgracefully ignorant, and continue to be so, lacking the sense of God's presence and all true knowledge of Him]. I say this to your shame. [35] But someone will say, How can the dead be raised? With what [kind of] body will they come forth? [36] You foolish man! Every time you plant seed, you sow something that does not come to life [germinating, springing up, and growing] unless it dies first. [37] Nor is the seed you sow then the body which it is going to have [later], but it is a naked kernel, perhaps of wheat or some of the rest of the grains. [38] But God gives to it the

body that He plans *and* sees fit, and to each kind of seed a body of its own.

Within the kingdom of God Yeshua refers to "seeds" as his people in order to describe the character that's being produced within them, (or in their heart) . It also states in the Bible the Seed is Christ word for word, look it up yourself. The Father was also speaking of Resurrection from the dead what body comes to life; He sees fit what is raised from death to life. Leviticus 12:2-4 explains also seed is people not money. Yeshua's kingdom speaks of a circumcised heart and character dying to self will and old ways, excepting the responsibility to change your immoral character and lusts of the flesh.

Luke 2:21-23 And at the end of eight days, when [the Baby] was to be circumcised, He was called Jesus, the name given by the angel before He was conceived in the womb.

22 And when the time for their purification [the mother's purification and the Baby's dedication] came according to the Law of Moses, they brought Him up to Jerusalem to present Him to the Lord—

23 As it is written in the Law of the Lord, Every [firstborn] male that opens the womb shall be set apart *and* dedicated *and* called holy to the Lord—

The Father wants us to be made Holy and live a life of sanctification; living set apart for His work and His glory. Most of us still believe that seed is money, in the Christ kingdom ministry bunch of purposeless talk of money, what a joke! Tithing is not Covenant that the New Testament speaks of, Romans 11:26-28 And so all Israel will be saved. As it is written, The Deliverer will come from Zion, He will banish ungodliness from Jacob. [27] And this will be My covenant (My agreement) with them when I shall take away their sins. [28] From the point of view of the Gospel (good news), they [the Jews, at present] are enemies [of God], which is for your advantage *and* benefit. But from the point of view of God's choice (of election, of divine selection), they are still the beloved (dear to Him) for the sake of their forefathers.

His covenant He speaks of is removing our iniquities, transgressions, sins and immoral character by the leading of the Holy Spirit. Psalms 103:12 As far as the east is from the west, so far has He removed our transgressions from us. Isaiah 30:1 Woe To the rebellious children, says the Lord, who take counsel *and* carry out a plan, but not Mine, and who make a league *and* pour out a drink offering, but not of My Spirit, thus adding sin to sin; Isaiah 30:9-12 For this is a rebellious people, faithless *and* lying sons, children who will

not hear the law *and* instruction of the Lord;
Speak to us what we want to hear , meaning
preach to us the hope of deceitfulness instead of
transformation. [10] Who [virtually] say to the seers
[by their conduct], See not! And to the prophets,
prophesy not to us what is right! Speak to us
smooth things, prophesy deceitful illusions. Last
[12] Therefore thus says the Holy One of Israel:
Because you despise *and* spurn this [My] word
and trust in cunning *and* oppression, in
crookedness *and* perverseness, and rely on them,

Have you ever noticed when leaders speak the
truth, or those who have gifts from the Father
Yahweh they do everything contradicting to what
they speak of. As long as they give you a ministers
position, using flattery like money or special
exultation in front of others for you to continue to
remain in the ministry. Most of you cannot or will
not consider these facts because you're searching
for position, acceptance and seeking to be used by
God no matter how it looks. The terms or
impregnation of being faithful in the little has
been transcribed within you to believe wait out
the outcome. You wouldn't know that you were
pulled or lured in by deceit totally blind to the
Demon Spirits tricks that these great leaders carry,
because they know you have no clue what
Discerning of Spirits is.

Saints, we need to recognize His loving caring transforming character within ourselves to be one with Him. Why is everyone so focused on His return, which is beautiful, but He wants a Bride purified in heart. If you're not transformed in your heart why would you want Him to come so soon? Rapture and Resurrection speaks of many forms of revelations. Can you not be rapture d in spirit, coming to an understanding that diagnoses you in some way to change and revolutionize you. Can you not be resurrected from false ignorance, are you really set free within your own soul and spirit.

The Book of Matthew speaks of sheep and goats; He specifically stated if we do not do these things he will thrust us to the eternal abyss. Matthew 25:33-46 And He will cause the sheep to stand at His right hand, but the goats at His left.

[34]Then the King will say to those at His right hand, Come, you blessed of My Father [you [g]favored of God and appointed to eternal salvation], inherit (receive as your own) the kingdom prepared for you from the foundation of the world.

[35] For I was hungry and you gave Me food, I was thirsty and you gave Me something to drink, I was a stranger and you [h]brought Me together with yourselves *and* welcomed *and* entertained *and [i]* lodged Me,

[36] I was naked and you clothed Me, I was sick and you visited Me [j]with help *and* ministering care, I was in prison and you came to see Me.

[37] Then the just *and* upright will answer Him, Lord, when did we see You hungry and gave You food, or thirsty and gave You something to drink?

[38] And when did we see You a stranger and welcomed *and* entertained You, or naked and clothed You?

[39] And when did we see You sick or in prison and came to visit You?

[40] And the King will reply to them, Truly I tell you, in so far as you did it for one of the least [[k]in the estimation of men] of these My brethren, you did it for Me.

[41] Then He will say to those at His left hand, be gone from Me, you cursed, into the eternal fire prepared for the devil and his angels!

[42] For I was hungry and you gave Me no food, I was thirsty and you gave Me nothing to drink,

[43] I was a stranger and you did not welcome Me *and* entertain Me, I was naked and you did not clothe Me, I was sick and in prison and you did not visit Me [l]with help *and* ministering care.

[44] Then they also [in their turn] will answer, Lord, when did we see You hungry or thirsty or a

stranger or naked or sick or in prison, and did not minister to You?

[45] And He will reply to them, Solemnly I declare to you, in so far as you failed to do it for the least [[m]in the estimation of men] of these, you failed to do it for Me.

[46] Then they will go away into eternal punishment, but those who are just *and* upright *and* in right standing with God into eternal life.

How many so called Christ believers or churches pass out money or even house the poor, it speaks of clothing the saints, aiding for food and shelter. Doesn't He say to house the poor or stranger in need, of course by the Leading of the Holy Spirit, feeding, sheltering and visiting those who are in prison. I have been involved in ministry for 17 years and never *have I* seen other so called Christians give out there hard working money to your brother or sister right next to them. Never have I seen congregations buying people cars or helping paying for driver's license or insurance for 6 months or anything that would aid their walk of life. Everyone is so concerned about lime light or the person behind the pulpit, now that was funny, the kingdom of Yahweh is all about Hospitality and Comfort. Do you notice Hospitals give out anything you need at the drop of a dime even if you don't have medical insurance. How come all of us Christians have this so called maturity and understanding of Yeshua's word and we cannot lift a finger for those in need. You will throw all your money for months into the offering basket to the leaders that are already living luxuriously but won't help out someone else to live luxuriously. Yeshua died on the cross, He bled spiritually for all mankind, that's what the Kingdom is about, bleeding for one another. Know those who labor among you, it also states those who pour out with money and material items to you.

ANTHONY MONTOYA

Chapter 2

In my walk of life to be quite honest; Omnish, Mormons, Muslims, Catholics, Chinese people who worship Buddha and other religions have aided me in hospitality, food, money and shelter, just like Yeshua describes in the Bible, way more than most Christians. There is no such thing as Church, its Kingdom at hand, there is no such thing as members of a certain ministry even though they profess it or ascribe to it or however it's implemented.

In God's kingdom to Him all were brothers, sisters and family, numb nuts! How retarded, how we ask each other what are you, what religion are you, what church do you go to, what member or group you're from. What happened to love, hospitality and accepting one another in love. Love one another as you love yourselves, I have received more comfort and joy in a bar than most churches. When I spoke of other religions or other people that had their own religion they actually bought cars, aided in shelter, rent homes for families, meaning they paid their rent for two years and food for months to those in need without asking for anything in return. They were just being Christ like to the tee!

Some of us have this understanding possibly that the coming of the day of the Lord is the rapture, taken up away from destruction. These appointed times is how He is coming Amos 5: 18-20 Woe to you who long for the day of the LORD! Why do you long for the day of the LORD? That day will be darkness, not light.[19] It will be as though a man fled from a lion only to meet a bear as though he entered his house and rested his hand on the wall only to have a snake bite him.[20] Will not the day of the LORD be darkness, not light— pitch-dark, without a ray of brightness?

The Father is bringing His justice and His destruction of His wrath upon mankind. Prophetically speaking a bear simplifies destruction of power or impact forcefully. Bears also indicate famine for food living without, aiding around for food and drought. Scripture then states to rest your hand on the wall only to have a snake bite, wound and strip you of your immunity responses.

False doctrine venom leaves you powerless, destroys your immunity response and attacks your confidence and self-esteem. Psalms 58:1-4 Do ye indeed speak righteousness, O congregation? Do ye judge uprightly, O ye sons of men? [2] Yea, in heart ye work wickedness; ye weigh the violence of your hands in the earth.[3] The wicked are estranged from the womb: they go astray as soon as they be born, speaking lies.[4] Their poison is like the poison of a serpent: they are like the deaf adder that stopped her ear. Matthew 16:12 Then understood they that He bade them not beware of the leaven of bread, but of the doctrine of the Pharisees and of the Sadducee s.

Now you're asking yourself why the Father would bring to us what is not good for us. Let's understand is it He that's asking, or us that's demanding from our hearts what's coming. Isaiah 65:11-13 But you who forsake the Lord, who forget *and* ignore My Holy Mount [Zion], who prepare a table for Gad [the Babylonian god of fortune] and who furnish mixed drinks for Meni [the god of destiny]—[12] I will destine you [says the Lord] for the sword, and you shall all bow down to the slaughter, because when I called, you did not answer; when I spoke, you did not listen *or* obey. But you did what was evil in My eyes, and you chose that in which I did not delight.[13] Therefore thus says the Lord God: Behold, My servants shall eat, but you shall be hungry; behold, My servants shall drink, but you shall be thirsty; behold, My servants shall rejoice, but you shall be put to shame.

We as believers possibly out of our ignorance, rebellion, and self-denial have made certain decisions in our hearts due to false impregnation, false hope; false prophecies that have wounded our hearts and ears that leave us crippled, sick and are totally blind to our own self-centeredness. We are saying prophecy to the idols of my heart for a price, the Spirit of influence has penetrated every part of ourselves, heart, body, mind, soul and spirit. Into our conscious, subconscious and seared conscious.

Family have you wondered why they talk so much about the Mark of the beast and all of its different doctrines of roads it leads to. The Mark of the Beast explained Revelation 13:17-18 So that no one will have power to buy or sell unless he bears the stamp (mark, inscription), [that is] the name of the beast or the number of his name.[18] Here is [room for] discernment [a call for the wisdom [d]of interpretation]. Let anyone who has intelligence (penetration and insight enough) calculate the number of the beast, for it is a human number [the number of a certain man]; his number is 666.

I will first show you where this is clarified from before I give you the prophetic revelation through the Holy Spirit. Some use carnal ways to justify our own responses, close and shut our ears and hearts due to the spirits we carry within ourselves to shut our ears up, the spirit of religion and influence.

42 U.S. Code § 666 - Requirement of statutorily prescribed procedures to improve effectiveness of child support enforcement:

(13) **Recording of social security numbers in certain family matters.** — Procedures requiring that the social security number of—

(A) Any applicant for a professional license, driver's license, occupational license, recreational license, or marriage license is recorded on the application;

(B) Any individual who is subject to a divorce decree, support order, or paternity determination or acknowledgment be placed in the records relating to the matter; and

(C) Any individual who has died be placed in the records relating to the death and be recorded on the death certificate.

For purposes of sub paragraph (A), if a State allows the use of a number other than the social security number to be used on the face of the document while the social security number is kept on file at the agency, the State shall so advise any applicants.

"He causes all, both small and great, rich and poor, free and slave, to receive a mark on their right hand or on their foreheads, and that no one may buy or sell, except one who has the mark or the name of the beast or the number of his name." Revelation 13:16-17. The social security card allows you to buy, sell and trade (people hello). Most of you don't know law, meaning you never read the law books where the truth comes from. Most attorneys do not tell you truth either; they have sworn an oath to protect the courts and Judges not the people.

Men of all nations have already received the Mark of the Beast long time ago! The Father also speaks of 2 more revelations regarding this verse the beastly carnal nature mentality of mankind!

The heavenly Father Speaks of the Gifts and talents of virtue and Purity! In the body of Christ Yeshua's kingdom the buying and selling the gifts and talents for influence, compromise, money, false doctrine laws, prostituting one another, selling each other like prostitutes, meat to share for a price, prostituting the virtue of our character and personalities for self-gain!........The Beastly mentality has to do with the spirit of Ignorance and stupor not being transparent; transparency in the motive and intentions of your heart! It's a title and law code Made by our government SSN card to buy, sell and trade. Happy now family, love you all, thank you all for your time and patience of reading, let's move on.

1 Timothy 1:7 Amplified

They are ambitious to be doctors of the Law (teachers of the Mosaic ritual), but they have no understanding either of the words *and* terms they use or of the subjects about which they make [such] dogmatic assertions.

Let me give you some more insight to this misunderstanding how new age philosophy, apostolic title ministers speak to what they have no clue what they speak of.

Revelation 17:10 the emperor Nero (They are also seven kings. Five have fallen, one is, the other has not yet come; but when he does come, he must remain for only a little while. The rule of the first seven Roman Emperors 1.Julius Caesar (49-44 BC) 2. Augustus (27 BC-AD 14) 3. Tiberius (AD 14-37 4. Caligula (AD 37-41) 5. Claudius (AD 41-54) one is still to come 6. Nero (AD 54-68) last only remained 7. Galba (June AD 68-January AD 69, a six month reign of ruler-ship).

IF you studied History, they called Nero a Beast because of his brutality of mind & massacres. CENTURIES B.C. [THE GREEK LETTERS USED IN SPELLING "NEBEKEDNESSER" ARE: NU (50!) + ETA (8) + BETA (2) + ETA (8) + KAPPA (20) + ETA (8) + DELTA (4) + NU (50) + ETA (8) + SIGMA (200) + SIGMA (200) + ETA (8) + RHO (100) = 666. Proof in Numerical Numerology.

In Ancient Times Rome was the source of market and retail, before you can pass the main gate you had to pay tribute and honor to the Idol Caesar, animals were sacrificed to pagan rituals even people and babies according to pagan traditions, then the ash was placed on the forehead or hand, then you would be allowed to pass through the gate.

The story refers to the Great Fire of Rome in AD 64 when half the city burnt to the ground. Nero seemed to have enjoyed the thrill of it all, and cared little about the city or the people. Afterward, when his popularity plummeted, he tried to salvage his reputation by blaming the Christians, and used their bodies as flaming torches to illuminate his gardens. Nero man of great evil, Jeremiah 27:3-6 And send them to the king of Edom, to the king of Moab, to the king of the Ammonites, to the king of Tyre, and to the king of Sidon by the hand of the messengers who have come to Jerusalem to Zedekiah king of Judah. [4] And command them to say to their masters, Thus says the Lord of hosts, the God of Israel: Thus shall you say to your masters: [5] I have made the earth, the men, and the beasts that are upon the face of the earth by My great power and by My outstretched arm, and I give it to whomever it seems right *and* suitable to Me. [6] And now I have given all these lands into the hand of

Nebuchadnezzar king of Babylon, My servant *and* instrument, and the beasts of the field also I have given him to serve him. Seven Kings also Babylonian and Egypt we also need to study history and events instead of using Gnosticism, religious utterances of philosophy, false doctrine anything that challenges a belief system that has no truth or bearing to it, your persecuted like democracy.

Saints, in the book of Isaiah it speak of General demons, Spirits powerless Ghosts, Mindsets Religious identities, Isaiah 26:13-14 O Lord, our God, other masters besides You have ruled over us, but we will acknowledge *and* mention Your name only. [14]They [the former tyrant masters] are dead, they shall not live *and* reappear; they are powerless ghosts, they shall not rise *and* come back. Therefore You have visited and made an end of them and caused every memory of them [every trace of their supremacy] to perish. The Bible speaks of Systems and spirits that have had Dominion over us, which means full control over your mindsets and thoughts, emotions, feelings, heart, body, mind, soul, and even your spirit man, the inner man.

Most systems are using the Good news for private gain, using you, feasting on your charity of giving, selling everything about God for a price changing it with Counterfeit influences. Matthew 24:23-26 If anyone says to you then, Behold, here is the Christ (the Messiah)! or, There He is!—do not believe it.

[24]For false Christ's and false prophets will arise, and they will show great signs and wonders so as to deceive *and* lead astray, if possible, even the elect (God's chosen ones) [25] See, I have warned you beforehand. [26] So if they say to you, Behold, He is in the wilderness (desert)—do not go out there; if they tell you, Behold, He is in the secret places *or* inner rooms—do not believe it.

What is this illustration saints ministry this church that church, special guest speaker, great name speaker, this house, this city, that state over here, meeting here conference here all the locusts have been flocking to it already and have been captured chained and bound! They sell and use you for a price and profit. Leviticus 19:31 Regard not them that have familiar spirits, neither seek after wizards, to be defiled by them: I *am* the LORD your God. In my first Book you read in the 2nd Testament of the Bible about the spirit of divination Acts 16:16-19 As we were on our way to the place of prayer, we were met by a slave girl who was possessed by a spirit of divination [claiming to foretell future events and to discover hidden knowledge], and she brought her owners much gain by her fortunetelling. [17] She kept following Paul and [the rest of] us, shouting loudly, These men are the servants of the Most High God! They announce to you the way of salvation! [18] And she did this for many days. Then Paul, being sorely annoyed *and* worn out, turned and said to the spirit within her, I charge you in the name of Jesus Christ to come out of her! And it came out that very moment. [19]But when her owners discovered that their hope of profit was gone, they caught hold of Paul and Silas and dragged them before the authorities in the forum (marketplace), [where trials are held].

You notice this spirit even spoke the truth about the Emissaries the Apostles, and Paul with the power of the Holy Spirit caught it in rebuked it out of her, she didn't even know she had it in her. Most Apostolic leaders today have these spirits within them, just because there prophesying in the name of The God, bringing much favor and gain to their hearers, moving in the gifts, there titles etc., just because a huge flock or locusts follow them.

Didn't you just read even it will confuse and deceive the elect that means, its generals even in the body of Christ. My beloved Saints, it states in the Bible to Run to the Mountains do not go back to even grab your coat. This is how serious it is life and death, polluting your very spirit to be caught and dragged down to complete destruction, to rule and reign in there democracy, compromise, complacency, being a part of their network sacrificing yourself to idols of witchery.

Chapter 3

Saints, lets jump to my first book if you have read it, I apologize for this brief inscription about the Tithe commandment of Law. I am going to illustrate to you a brief inscription that details some red flags about Tithing. Acts 4:36-37 Now Joseph, a Levite (Priest) and native of Cyprus who was surnamed Barnabas by the apostles, which interpreted, means Son of Encouragement.

[37] Sold a field which belonged to him and brought the sum of money and laid it at the feet of the apostles. You notice if you have read the 1stTestament of the Bible which is the old Covenant or 1st Testament, 12 tribes of Israel, God speaks to the Nation of Israel only; the Levites were the high priests that would sacrifice animals on the altar for the forgiveness of sins for the nation of Israel. Now you're asking yourself, what significance is this. Let's proceed, did you know what the Levite had to do to enter the Holy of Hollies.

The tabernacle of the Israelite's was a highly restricted area. Only Aaron and his descendants were allowed inside the tabernacle to offer sacrifices. (Aaron was a Levite—that is, a descendant of Jacob's son Levi. To be a priest, one must be a Levite. On the other hand, not all Levites were priests. Only a particular family of Levites, the Kohathites, could become priests. Other Levites, however, were involved in the maintenance and transport of the tabernacle). Penalties for violating access to the tabernacle and its contents were so severe as to result in leprosy or death. Certain rituals inside the tabernacle were so specific that improper administration likewise resulted in death (Leviticus 10:1-7).

Levites followed rules beyond recognition to the tee! Or they ended up with leprosy or death. You notice Joseph did not give a certain percentage or tenth to the apostles feet. There has been a new covenant that the Priest witnessed, about a way better covenant than the old one. Why would Joseph not Tithe according to his laws knowing anything that he does can result in some dramatic fatality or disease. Notice Joseph gave instead of the law tenth or tithe. See reference, Hebrews 8:13

Saints, God said the first Covenant is now old, obsolete (out of use). He has made a New Covenant to all Mankind. Read Hebrews 7:5 (Tithe was commandment and law) Hebrews 7:12 (When there is a new high priest there is a change and alteration of the law) Hebrews 7:18 (The regulation and command is canceled) other Bibles

(The regulation or command is dis annulled). Dis annulled- Dictionary-make void, to cancel. Saints, when you write a check out and you cancel it, do you not write the Inscription (VOID) on the check.

Saints and family, thank you for your precious time and patience. Let's move on, Romans 8:23-25 Not only so, but we ourselves, who have the (first fruits) of the Spirit, groan inwardly as we wait eagerly for our adoption to Son ship, the redemption of our bodies. [24] For in this hope we were saved. But hope that is seen is no hope at all. Who hopes for what they already have? [25] But if we hope for what we do not yet have, we wait for it patiently.

Now what does this clarify well, according to Levitical Jewish times It would be considered that, under the Levitical dispensation, the Lord commanded that the first-fruits, in the form of a single sheaf, should be sickle, and waved before him by the priest;(Notice it was only the priest) that this wave-offering was to be considered as constituting the herald or the pledge of a ripened and full harvest. And not only should it be an earnest and a pledge, but it should represent the nature and character of the fruit which, before long, in luxury abundance would crowd with its golden sheaves, and amid shouts of gladness, the swelling garner.

Now Saints considering the tithe aspect, only the Levite which was one of the 12 tribes of Israel were expected to Tithe; notice there tithing was also a covenant and connection to blessings. Why? Because none of them had the Holy Spirit of communication and none of the 11 tribes talked to God in the Holy of Hollies hello....In the first Testament this was the connection, now what does the First fruit of increase become or became. The Holy Spirit and Yeshua's blood, now you have direct access to God for communication, sanctification, the Holy Spirit has the power to break strongholds, curses, bondage's everything. Acts 7:51-53 "You stiff-necked people! Your hearts and ears are still uncircumcised. You are just like your ancestors: You always resist the Holy Spirit! [52] Was there ever a prophet your ancestors did not persecute? They even killed those who predicted the coming of the Righteous One. And now you have betrayed and murdered him— [53] you who have received the law that was given through angels but have not obeyed it."

It stated you people reject and resist the Holy Spirit, you do not want the edification of speaking in tongues which is no language any man can understand, and you don't want the Holy Spirit to work with the sword of the spirit to penetrate to the depths of your inner core of your heart because spiritually it's beyond painful. Hebrews

10:31 it is a dreadful thing to fall into the hands of the living God. He Yahweh is a consuming Fire; you all can communicate with Yahweh, the throne through the Holy Spirit. People in general have made a decision in their hearts or been deceived that your tithe is the direct access and has the power to break strongholds. I do believe in your adoration and love for God in giving money for the sake of the kingdom of God. Your First fruits is no longer the tithe because you all now have direct access for anything you need. Some of you continue to want a Task Master, also want others to go into the Holy Hollies and come out then pray for me or use the gift to give me what's needed. Secondly you all been blinded by false theology and religious doctrine making you feel you're not worthy enough to receive the gifts of God. Oh no really, then why are so called church members still sitting under their task masters for more than 3-5-10-15 years in the same Church organization, ministry, etc. Without any gifts no mantles waiting for your task master to tell you when you're ready, that was funny.

We have forgotten a lot about focusing of Hospitality, the religious spirit looks at others through monetary items & wealth, then questioning where your prosperity is then if you speak the truth. Paul the Apostle the emissary 2

Corinthians 6:3-10 We put no obstruction in anybody's way [we give no offense in anything], so that no fault may be found *and* [our] ministry blamed *and* discredited. [4] But we commend ourselves in every way as [true] servants of God: through great endurance, in tribulation *and* suffering, in hardships *and* privations, in sore straits *and* calamities, [5] In beatings, imprisonments, riots, labors, sleepless watching, hunger; [6] By innocence *and* purity, knowledge *and* spiritual insight, long suffering *and* patience, kindness, in the Holy Spirit, in unfeigned love; [7] By [speaking] the word of truth, in the power of God, with the weapons of righteousness for the right hand [to attack] and for the left hand [to defend]; [8] Amid honor and dishonor; in defaming *and* evil report and in praise *and* good report. [We are branded] as deceivers (impostors), and [yet vindicated as] truthful *and* honest. [9] [We are treated] as unknown *and* ignored [by the world], and [yet we are] well-known *and* recognized [by God and His people]; as dying, and yet here we are alive; as chastened by suffering and [yet] not killed; [10] As grieved *and* mourning, yet [we are] always rejoicing; as poor [ourselves, yet] bestowing riches on many; as having nothing, and [yet in reality] possessing all things.

Wait just a minute Paul & the apostles stated out of all these hardships he was poor and hungry, really how could this be in the book of Acts 4:1-4 And while they [Peter and John] were talking to the people, the high priests and the military commander of the temple and the Sadducee s came upon them, [2] Being vexed *and* indignant through *and* through because they were teaching the people *and* proclaiming in [the case of] Jesus the resurrection from the dead. [3] So they laid hands on them (arrested them) and put them in prison until the following day, for it was already evening. [4] But many of those who heard the message believed (adhered to and trusted in and relied on Jesus as the Christ). And their number grew *and* came to about 5,000.

Did you just read this, 5,000 Jews and Gentiles were added to their ministry, if the tithe was preached to them or administered about tithing, how then could the 12 apostles be hungry or poor. Tithing was not preached or administered at all in the New Testament or 2nd Testament Folks. I hope and pray with love you all got the understanding. When I speak of 1st testament and 2nd I am referring to the old covenant and new covenant, but many of Yahweh's word is still the same. Let me give you a few Divine nuggets of increase and favor.

In the book of Galatians 4:8-10 in its entire form, But at that previous time, when you had not come to be acquainted with *and* understand *and* know the true God, you [Gentiles] were in bondage to gods who by their very nature could not be gods at all [gods that really did not exist].

[9] Now, however, that you have come to be acquainted with *and* understand *and* know [the true] God, or rather to be understood *and* known by God, how can you turn back again to the weak and beggarly *and* worthless elementary things [[d]of all religions before Christ came], whose slaves you once more want to become?

[10] You observe [particular] days and months and seasons and years!

Saints, we are no longer bound by the elements of nature or the carnal nature of mankind, you notice in the book of Romans 6 :5-6 For if we have become one with Him by sharing a death like His, we shall also be [one with Him in sharing] His resurrection [by a new life lived for God].

[6] We know that our old (unrenewed) self was nailed to the cross with Him in order that [our] body [which is the instrument] of sin might be made ineffective *and* inactive for evil, that we might no longer be the slaves of sin.

Let me explain the elements of this world, were not bound by time or any Nero genetic conditions of natural intelligence or science, only of Yeshua and the Holy Spirit within us. Also, in school we were raised, the system even taught us backwards ways of thinking, like so Who, What, When, Where, Why and also the How benefactor. In Gods kingdom there's no questioning just obedience, trust and believing is knowing, We should have been trained as follows, Origin, Process, Completion, Will, purpose and define definitions for specific instruction more greatly understood.

In the book of 1 Peter 1:23 you have been regenerated (born again), not from a mortal [d]origin ([e]seed, sperm), but from one that is immortal by the *ever* living and lasting Word of God. Wow it states we have been regenerated by one that is immortal lasting living word of Yahweh. 1 Peter 4:9-10 Practice hospitality to one another (those of the household of faith). [Be hospitable, be a lover of strangers, with brotherly affection for the unknown guests, the foreigners, the poor, and all others who come your way who are of Christ's body.] And [in each instance] do it ungrudging (cordially and graciously, without complaining but as representing Him).

[10] As each of you has received a gift (a particular spiritual talent, a gracious divine endowment), employ it for one another as [befits] good trustees of God's many-sided grace [faithful stewards of

the [f]extremely diverse powers and gifts granted to Christians by unmerited favor].

My beloved Saints above all it states the practicing of Hospitality, to the lost, strangers, unknown guests, the foreigners and the poor and all others who come your way of who are of Yeshua's body. Now giving us an escalating transition, showing hospitality without complaining and with grace without grudgingly. The Bible speaks of those who are not part or member of a congregation, other religions, strangers and the poor. It also implements if those of a divine gift a particular spiritual talent, it being employed for one another as a proper benefit for those in need.

I'm going to put it down the way Yeshua's describes it, so special people think they need to be praised or paid to such services or make others feel obligated to something in return for them. Luke 14:12-14 Jesus also said to the man who had invited Him, when you give a dinner or a supper, do not invite your friends or your brothers or your relatives or your wealthy neighbors, lest perhaps they also invite you in return, and so you are paid back.

[13] But when you give a banquet or a reception, invite the poor, the disabled, the lame, and the blind.

¹⁴ Then you will be blessed (happy, fortunate, and [c]to be envied), because they have no way of repaying you, and you will be recompensed at the resurrection of the just (upright).

Have you noticed so called Christians always treat their friends, brothers and relatives or wealthy neighbors with some kind of formal hospitality, but will not lift a finger for the lost, disabled, lame and blind. Yeshua's kingdom spoke as stated do not worry about being repaid for any of your services but do it unto the King with compassion and admirable service for free & not for self gain. You notice the lame, sick, blind, crippled, disabled and blind normally do not have anything to repay back to you. You are probably asking yourself where am I going with all this, your reading it word for word what happened to the true nature of Yeshua's kingdom, not all this human regulations and commands that the body of Christ gives to those in need a membership application. Telling them or asking dumb questions like are you tithing, do you have a home church, do you have a Pastor, what church you go to, are you fasting enough, what you do for a living or pinpointing your weaknesses why you're not succeeding in life.

Chapter 4

Romans 6:3-5 says, Are you ignorant of the fact that all of us who have been baptized into Christ Jesus were baptized into His death?

[4] We were buried therefore with Him by the baptism into death, so that just as Christ was raised from the dead by the glorious [power] of the Father, so we too might [habitually] live *and* behave in newness of life.

[5] For if we have become one with Him by sharing a death like His, we shall also be [one with Him in sharing] His resurrection [by a new life lived for God]. It specifically states we will shall share in the same likeness as his death and be resurrected in the same likeness as His resurrection. My beloved children we need to watch for the words we speak. Does it not state in the Bible (Man shall not live by bread alone but by every word that proceeds out of the mouth of God). In the Book of Proverbs 18:20 English Standard Version. From the fruit of a man's mouth his stomach is satisfied; he is satisfied by the yield of his lips. New American Standard Bible.

With the fruit of a man's mouth his stomach will be satisfied; He will be satisfied with the product of his lips. In other cases a man is satisfied by the consequences of his own tongue. My beloved children agelessness is a gift from the heavens. If you continue to speak that you're getting old and declare your birthdays and bound by the year cycle (God) then you get what you speak. We shall be resurrected in the same likeness as His resurrection. At the end of Galatians it states we have full freedom in the spirit, cast out the bond woman and become one of the free promises of unlimited access to His divine wisdom, revelation and understanding.

Oh really where is that in the Bible, alright Isaiah 65:20-22 There shall no more be in it an infant who lives but a few days, or an old man who dies prematurely; for the child shall die a hundred years old, and the sinner who dies when only a hundred years old shall be [thought only a child, cut off because he is] accursed.

^{21} They shall build houses and inhabit them, and they shall plant vineyards and eat the fruit of them.

^{22} They shall not build and another inhabit; they shall not plant and another eat [the fruit]. For as the days of a tree, so shall be the days of My people, and My chosen *and* elect shall long make use of *and* enjoy the work of their hands. It specifically indicates that the days of my people or as the trees, trees live how long, yes you got it hundreds of years 6oo to 1000 years long. One more verse to clarify your understanding saints **Psalm 71:9** cast **me not of**f *nor* send **me** away **in the time of old age**; forsake **me not** when my strength is spent *and* my powers fail.

The Father Yahweh has granted us favor to live longer, yes if we eat right, you notice Japan came up with Alkaline water at 9.5, the water bottles we drink are what 7.8 Ph. in the stores. If you go and study Alkaline water your drinking pure oxygen you never had since birth. More and more citizens are starting to eat organic food it's on demand, mankind is figuring out companies' tricks of what is produced in our drinks and foods. My beloved saints we are being rapture d into the likeness of His own kind, the way He walks, thinks and moves not the way of the world, but yes we will remain earthly good in character and wise. Yeshua's compassion drives Him through His own Fathers love, will and kind intentions for all mankind.

In my walk I went to one service where a beloved brother introduced to me the understanding of increase where money did not move the power of God. In the book of Luke 7:11-15 [c] Soon afterward, Jesus went to a town called Nain, and His disciples and a great throng accompanied Him.

[12] [Just] as He drew near the gate of the town behold, a man who had died was being carried

out—the only son of his mother, and she was a widow; and a large gathering from the town was accompanying her.

¹³ And when the Lord saw her, He had compassion on her and said to her, do not weep.

¹⁴ And He went forward and touched the funeral bier, and the pallbearers stood still. And He said, Young men, I say to you, arise [[d]from death]!

¹⁵ And the man [who was] dead sat up and began to speak. And [Jesus] gave him [back] to his mother.

You notice in this passage I thought it was nothing but short of a miracle from the dead. There was more illustration of great promise, if you also study history in its perspective; the widows were very poor and the sons were the bread winners in the family. When Yeshua gave back the widow her son he gave her increase, finances, joy etc., for free not asking the woman if she was a tither, how dumb. Yeshua and the apostles moved in demonstration and power never once asking the person in front of them in aid for a membership application or if they were tithers at all. When I received this revelation of increase wells opened up within my very being I felt it so strong. The book of Psalms declares His glorious understanding of revelation Psalms 1:1 How blessed are those who reject the advice of the wicked, don't stand on the way of sinners or sit where scoffers sit! [2] Their delight is in ADONAI's *Torah*; on His *Torah* they meditate day and night. [3] They are like trees planted by streams —they bear their fruit in season, their leaves never wither, everything they do succeeds. When you study His word by Revelation on His word everything you do you shall have success, it's all in His word not parapsychology references of Greek, pagan understanding, myths, fables, genealogies, fairy tales, false doctrine, reading a script from the Bible and thinks it was a great sounding word with no Holy Spirit in it.

There have been many expressions on what we consider life, obstacles and transitions; everyone has presented themselves to reach a certain goal to prosper in life. In the kingdom we need to be stripped from all things, for Yeshua to become all in all within us. Yes, even the unction of wanting to achieve and prosper needs to be ripped out of your mortal spirits. Now you're asking yourself what does this mean, or how can you say such a thing. How can you really find rest within yourself if Yeshua and the Holy Spirit don't have complete control over you? I believe there are those who have had experiences of Yahweh favoring them because they fasted or tithed many times and everyone has great testimonies. In my experiences in life through ministry and my earthly walk, is about living your life sacrificially for the sake of the kingdom. We are also clearly not to be connected to immoral brother hood that are not in transparency.

You notice in the Bible when Yeshua healed the ten leaper's only one person returned to thank Yeshua for what was given to him. Yeshua or the Apostles never placed burdens on anyone at all, but for everyone to make a choice to lay their own self wills at the cross. Sometimes we tend to want to pinpoint the answer or the reason why certain things happen, life teaches you there's got to be an answer to everything, or you get all logical. In the system you come up with assumptions or beliefs and you make them concrete to identify the criteria or situation at hand. Never asking the Holy Spirit for aid or guidance, possibly because you want to be heard or someone to understand you when you speak. We have many formalities to deal with for a divine presence to deliver us from ourselves completely.

We all have heard the term hear no evil, speak no evil, see no evil, which is a good way to live. Communication of humanism or behaviorism expresses its conduits interchangeably. We all need to understand Agape love or empathy unconditional love like never before then and only then can we perceive to see things with much greater height and depth of His Spirit, Yeshua. The Holy Spirit was the best thing given to mankind. I believe everything has to do with the revelation of His word in mysteries and revelations.

Proverbs 25:2 (Specifically states a King searches out the truth, not just the wisdom & knowledge but the understanding of it all to find out).

The Heavenly Father and the Holy Spirit spoke to me in the Month of May 2014 about what is taking place. Zechariah 13:1-6

Amplified Bible (AMP)

[1] In that day there shall be a fountain opened for the house of David and for the inhabitants of Jerusalem [to cleanse them from] sin and uncleanness.

[2] And in that day, says the Lord of hosts, I will cut off the names of the idols from the land, and they shall no more be remembered; and also I will remove from the land the [false] prophets and the unclean spirit.

[3] And if anyone again appears [falsely] as a prophet, then his father and his mother who bore him shall say to him, you shall not live, for you speak lies in the name of the Lord; and his father and his mother who bore him shall thrust him through when he prophesies.

⁴ And in that day the [false] prophets shall each be ashamed of his vision when he prophesies, nor will he wear a hairy *or* rough garment to deceive,

⁵ But he will [deny his identity and] say, I am no prophet. I am a tiller of the ground, for I have been made a bond servant from my youth.

⁶ And one shall say to him, what are these wounds on your breast *or* between your hands? Then he will answer those with which I was wounded [when disciplined] in the house of my [loving] friends.

The Heavenly Father is bringing truth to this land of Earth. He is going to put an end to false truth and all its impurities that come along with it. I am going to explain where demonic activity or strongholds also appear in ministry. Such leaders call their congregations to bind up elements such as spirits against the nation or city.

You cannot enter into spiritual warfare without the leading of the Holy Spirit. This opens up attack on the congregation, yes you can pray for strongholds to be broken over family and those around you or in your circle of need. Doesn't it state specifically to pray like this (Our father in heaven) Matthew 6:9-13. If you're going to pray against the nation or the city and the Holy Spirit does not give you intercession access or leading you pray for the sins of the city or nation and stand in the gape for them and their ancestry forefathers.

You notice in the Bible Many prophets were to pray for the sins of the city or nation, they did not enter into spiritual warfare against the prince generals of the atmosphere, repentance is the answer for sins.

Ezekiel 4:4 "Then lies on your left side and put the sin of the people of Israel upon you. You are to bear their sin for the number of days you lie on your side. He had to lie on his side for a year to bear the sins of the people. We need the Holy Spirit to strategically call on aid to see into the enemy's camp and demolish it with divine instructions!

Some of you continue to have an illustration about fasting, yes it works I do agree, but let me give you some understanding to the Scriptures about this. Yes, in the book of the Bible there's a situation where the Apostles could not cast this spirit out and only Yeshua could. Yeshua did specifically state you can only do this by prayer and fasting. Here is why, when Yeshua gave the command to His work, they went in His power of the command in His name and His word! The Apostles at one point in time could not cast out such a spirit upon one human being because they did not have the Holy Spirit yet! Hello, they went in the power of

His name; Yeshua did not die on the cross yet, to give us the Holy Spirit. Yeshua was able to it because He already had the Holy Spirit in him, hello!

I need to remind you its about Discipline, obedience and transformation to know the Holy Spirit to do the work. Also, about your motives and intentions of your heart, it's all about obedience of His specific instructions, we all need divine healing. In ministry some of us put on our two face masks, yes we all know what that means, we can fake a personality or character very easily for years. I was at a service and was lead by the Spirit about healing in these two ladies bodies that were crying out for healing. One had kidney problems and the other lady her liver. They were told to stay away from heavy sugar; here get this, after they were prayed for and the service ended they grabbed a plate and put cheesecake, chocolate cookies, brownies with a salad covered in heavy dressing.

You know what that sounds like; we do not listen or take heed to instructions very well do we? We all need discipline and most important the Holy Spirit and His love more than ever. In the Holy Bible it does speak of one of the attributes of long suffering, we need to fall in love with this character. Yes, in many experiences there has been trials and tribulations, there's is a point in references to our walk where it comes to an end. Let me clarify this in Scripture the book of Isaiah 51:21-23 (Therefore, now hear this, you who are afflicted, and [who are] drunk, but not with wine [but thrown down by the wrath of God].

22 Thus says your Lord, the Lord, and your God, Who pleads the cause of His people: Behold, I have taken from your hand the cup of staggering *and* intoxication; the cup of My wrath you shall drink no more.

23 And I will put it into the hands of your tormentors *and* oppressors, those who said to you, Bow down, that we may ride *or* tread over you; and you have made your back like the ground and like the street for them to pass over). The Fathers wrath and His hand specifically come from Him alone. Isaiah 51:19 states there was double calamities came upon us, ruin, destruction, famine and sword. There comes a point where He reverses His trials and testings on us through the Baptism of Fire!

The book of Psalms 119:27 (Let me understand the teaching of Your precepts then I will meditate on Your wonders). Many shall come to the knowledge or searching of it but will never come into the metamorphosis of a transformed heart and character of the truth within. Let me give you more Revelation of how we are made in His image. In the book of Proverbs 18:21 (Death & life are in the power of the tongue). What was the Ark of the Covenant Resembling (You notice the ark has two angels on each side, your mouth left side is one wing, the other is the second wing). Faith comes by Hearing of the word of God so it can germinate within your heart to be transformed, your left ear has this shape and your right ear has the other half, two ears shapes put them to together it has the shape of an heart. Last but not least, in the book of the Bible **Revelation 4:6 And before the throne there was a sea of glass like unto crystal: and in the midst of the throne, and round about the throne, were four beasts full of eyes before and behind.**

If you studied the brain there's a fluid called cerebral aqueduct. Etymology: L, *cerebrum* + *aqueduct's,* water canal. The narrow conduit in the mid brain, between the third and the fourth ventricles, that conveys cerebrospinal fluid. Also called **aqueduct of Sylvius**. Three injunctions, Just like The Father, the Son, the Holy Spirit made in His image and likeness. Yes my beloved children we are made from Dust from our forefathers, but um let me clarify something, were made from Holy fire and spoken word, were you made from dust, or were you made from an embryonic seed embryo hello, not dust!

I have come up an illustration called mesmoractic cells, have not yet been discovered but let me help you understand this scenario, have you ever watched a movie and a young child witnesses a murder or drastic situation and scared out of his or hers wits. The child seems fine after months of relaxing, but when a psychologist comes into helping them bring back the memory they seem traumatized, cry, convulse, and possibly lead to brain disorders or malfunctions within the body somehow. I have come up with some illustrations of the councils five origins; you have Atmospheric messages, Encryption codes, Web filters, Mesmoractic cells, Black dust. I am going to explain each one in detail.

First one; Atmospheric messages- Prophecy parallel universe, also when someone has a great title or name whenever they speak they have great influence helping to change the mindsets or overcoming their own wills to make a choice. When someone speaks you're giving them a legitimate intervention, for the hearer to reach its own council within, you being a voice in the air and a statement on the table. Second; Encryption codes- information that leads to revelations, mysteries, new ideas, new inventions etc. Third; Web filters- Clouds of smoke, false impregnation, false prophecies, lies, poison eggs hatched in your spirit, false hope, in the spirit realm many religious doctrine being spoken like webbed like filters, just like a spun spider web, these announcements shoot spider webs at you behind the pulpit and attach them to your souls and spirits, why because your still human and have biological systems that are still at work within you that you cannot understand. I have personally been to numerous meetings where a Prophet or Apostle prophecy to an individual and specifically state you have been feed poison, you have been prophesied dogmatic witchcraft over you and this poison was not of God.

Leader's that already know how to move in the realm of the spirit just like star wars the Jedi, there were only few, knew how to maneuver this gift, why do you think there's many different congregations, many systems of orthodox and we all read mainly from the same Bible. But every congregation picks and chooses what to administer. These webs filter your spirit until they are deceased and vaporized. Fourth; you have Mesmoractic cells, you have subconscious, seared conscious and regular conscious, I have personally been introduced to a situation where a woman that had the trust of her family, but her family member manipulated and deceived her trust and twisted it for his own evil. When someone is traumatized, I also call it trauma memory cells, when there is too much control going on, pick pulling, she began to get welts on her forehead two lumps or bumps, she was confused on life, and could not understand direction. Her own father told me, yes I went to visit him, he said we don't tell her what to do with his eyes blood shot red and his face with condemnation all over it, pointing his eyes to the ground the whole time he was speaking. Nero physics or interrogation methods explain when someone tells a lie there eyes shut or they look left or right or completely look at the ground and cannot look at you eye to eye, their physiology signals are all off, even their pupils dilating to different sizes.

Her forehead started to create what you call memory cells, clouds of dust and smoke, like a memory bubble, a few months later the truth was revealed, she was forced out of her house, she called me and stated her father kicked her out of the house with her six year old child, I told her how come you didn't call social services, she told me over the phone her dad said if she was going to call he would lie to them. He had manipulated and deceived her and made her to completely fear him psychologically. A few months later the memory cells or memory bubbles disappeared overtime in a few months when she received care and aid from her mother side of the family. She went to live with her mom and grandparents who live in the same house. Fifth; I call it Black dust- Motive and intentions of the heart, conditions of the heart, you have multi personality issues, a couple revealed to me that her husband, yes she was a prophetess, the Holy Spirit said he had 22 different personalities, he was raised in the navy or army, he was in special forces, go figure where they came from. Highly intelligent icons of the master mind, which also deals with the heart.

Here is another element I created, which enables how the Holy Spirit works or how con figurative where information comes to unity. EAM= Entrapment- O symbol as a circle or whole, surrounding and capturing on all sides. The Bible speaks He wants to make us whole again, to become complete rest within. Assumptive closure- . Symbol dot, the Bible speaks we are the apple of His eye. Its meaning formulated His announcement is so confidently true to make the other perspective true or cannot be denied. Third; M- form of a cloud Moisture, marketing cells, wavelength signal, I also call it His Shekinah Glory, Nuclear magnetic resonance signaling. The submarines used in our armed forces when they receive a signal it's called an EAM alert transmission. You can possibly unite this with Nuclear Physics.

As I was explaining Scientific intelligence states we have billions of brain cells within the mind unicellular(conscious), intro-cellular (sub conscious), when we create more cells within our brain where does the other cells go, I believe it's called dense matter infinite space (Seared conscious). 1st Timothy 4:1-4 But the [Holy] Spirit distinctly *and* expressly declares that in latter times some will turn away from the faith, giving attention to deluding *and* seducing spirits and doctrines that demons teach. [2] Through the hypocrisy *and* pretensions of liars whose consciences are seared (cauterized), Neurotransmitters- 60 trillion flex compositors. Neurons – 100 billion diamond clusters.

Intelligence states when looked at they are diamond shaped clusters. Doesn't it state in the book of the Bible Yeshua walked on water, He became what midst, a dense cloud of midst. That's how valuable everyone is beyond our own understanding. Go look at how a Neurotransmitter works, we are not all connected there's an element called synoptic space, that shoots signals form one point to another. I believe were made of spiritually glory and fire!

Watch your words what you speak, ask the Father to show you a self revelation of yourself, to be delivered and completely healed. Anyone one of us can harm or hurt someone, even ourselves. The ultimate answer is the Holy Spirit. Why do you think a lot of us jump from congregations to others, or cell to cell groups, always learning and expressing, moving and demonstrated with no Holy Spirit orchestration. Never can become completely delivered and strong wiled to the Holy Spirit, well, you know what they say attitude dictate leadership. In the form of Religion, look how strong atmospheric messages are being produced everywhere, winds of doctrine cycles etc. The Bible states to guard your heart, put on your armor daily, just like you take care of your hygiene daily same thing. Organize, become proper, clean your room, vehicle, purses etc. Everything happens in the Natural before the spiritual first, yes find out it's in the Bible look for it. I believe I already gave the Scripture. Read 1 Corinthians 15:46-52 the whole chapter several times. [46] But it is not the spiritual life which came first, but the physical and then the spiritual. [47] Now those who are made of the dust are like him who was first made of the dust (earthly-minded); and as is [the Man] from heaven, so also [are those] who are of heaven (heavenly-minded).

[49] And just as we have borne the image [of the man] of dust, so shall we *and so* [g]*let us* also bear the image [of the Man] of heaven.

[51] Take notice! I tell you a mystery (a secret truth, an event decreed by the hidden purpose or counsel of God). We shall not all fall asleep [in death], but we shall all be changed (transformed)

[52] In a moment, in the twinkling of an eye, at the [sound of the] last trumpet call. For a trumpet will sound, and the dead [in Christ] will be raised imperishable (free and immune from decay), and we shall be changed (transformed).

You truly believe we are going anywhere yet, I believe soon maybe in the next 15 to 25 years, why you say, and well for one thing we or none of us are walking in, the likeness and manner of Yeshua's people yet. There are Dimensions of course, what's the first; well we see in the Bible it state your sons and daughters shall see dreams and visions and shall prophecy ok. We all have dreams and visions. Third; is prophecy in different formalities of coming to pass long term, short term, or within 24 hours or three days. Gifts of Inner Healing and Deliverance. Then you have Yeshua going to the other side, He came against the Principality of the General demons of cities and nations. This is only specifically used if the Holy Spirit gives you the specific instructions how to come against the Principalities of the Generals in cities and nations. You also have made time stand still, when it comes to nature's course, just like the spirit of Elijah. Then you have Yeshua walking on water, and then you have Him translated from one place to another.

Now some of you may have encountered a rapture to be taken away, really, most of the body of Christ is not walking in Conquer ship mode like Yeshua walks, not even close. Second; doesn't the word state we shall be transformed, meaning into new levels of mystery revelations, information's of unity coming from the heavens through Melchizedek the angel on the Ark of the Covenant. Last trumpet, what does a trumpet signify, it means Prophets and Apostles the message, the new mysteries of information. We shall be raptured in spirit metaphorically. Not raptured away to leave this earth, at least not yet. Yes, my beloved children and saints, the two angels on the Ark of the Covenant was Lucifer himself and the other was Melchizedek. Let me explain Melchizedek was explaining as having no father or mother lineage, not human, an angel , well Lucifer Deceived 1/3 of the angels of heaven how, he convinced the other angels, I will allow you to see fit and see the mysteries and treasures on this side of heaven. Lucifer had access to this storehouse, but what did he do, he prostituted his treasure for self glory, selling it for a price, he told the angels look through me and not Yahweh Himself.

Melchizedek means (King)-(Righteousness) He is like a mighty rushing river flowing. Constantly granting Favor, scrolls, information, gifts, and treasures of this access to the heavens. Wells of Favor and everything else, access to the treasures of heaven. I got this part of information through a Prophet Andre Hardin, thank you brother love you. Some of you have this doctrine about Tithing, read the Bible correctly Abraham gave a tenth of his assets from the spoils of war, not from his own income he received. This is where tithing has been twisted my beloved, read the Bible correctly. No such thing as Tithing, Saints and children hello.

I was recently at a service where a young 16 year old girl had an encounter that rattled her, she told me she stated that I am somerholer (A man who plays a role in vampire diaries TV show) he is my husband and were going to get married. Now she has his photos on the wall, her i-phone, t-shirt etc. Two weeks ago in the month of June she actually levitated off of her bed and she said she also sees black shadows passing. I told her she comes through a bloodline of Prophets, she's called to be a seer and the anointing on her is heavy. I told her she made a covenant speech with her tongue and that's how powerful our words are. I told her to renounce the covenant she had made, and advised her even ornaments or gifts hold demonic influence when there prayed over also or made even if they represent some demonic symbol or attached spiritually.

Family we need to be careful what we speak, why gossip or cause division, its possibly your the problem within your own self. How you may ask, well why is it everyone jumps from church to church or meetings to meetings constantly, one you don't take heed to Gods instructions or your already impregnated with false doctrine and many viruses of it planted or resonating within you. You continue to have ungodly soul ties in ministry, these friends you have known over 5,10 to 20 years are involved in major ministries and you give your complete trust to them. Somehow they break their trust with you and also continue to use you for their own private gain. I understand but lets be real, you continue in your own ignorance because you say to yourself well they believe in it and their doing it also. So you commune with whatever their involved in or beliefs are. Why you say because your lonely and possibly insecure in some areas within you, yes my beloved saints admit it.

Religion carries a witchery spirit, comparing and competing and causing division everywhere they go. One illustration of an incident few months ago as recent, a major prophet who I honor has a gift of Healing and deliverance very heavy. I myself in all humility brought him over 18 people to his home for fellowship, he was holding meetings once a week. His intentions were not what he spoke of when we had an agreement it all changed the minute his house filled up once a week. He started to manifest and lash at me with all his religious doctrine and wanted me to submit under his covering. He or the spirit within him starting using psychology or parapsychology interpretations when speaking to me about him controlling me. I told him out of love he was lost and blind and revealed to him what his intentions were how they switched and what areas in his life he needed alignment and why he was acting and speaking this way or form of mannerism. He couldn't handle it and manifested even the more. Yes I told him love you but I'm separating myself from you and cannot continue to be involved in that circle of mistrust.

Chapter 5

Saints I am revealing to you how the human gender operates when mixture is polluted within your spirit about doctrine and religion. It totally blinds your response of spirit and immune system, most leaders cant stand correction, the bible speaks iron sharpens iron, prophets are subject to the spirit of prophets. Saints you must be ready at all time to guard your heart, another incident accrued in this same circle, one woman was told numerous times who has an intercession spirit and very anointed. She has been healed of many things in her whole life, a prophet told her she needs to stop looking to be accepted in a ministry and wait on God for the commission and calling. I recently found out this woman gossiped constantly about everyone when she wasn't honored or uplifted in the ministry homes or services. She wanted to have a say so in everything, she was looking for a position and not waiting on God. Saints I'm revealing this incident to open your eyes, the false humility gender of spirit, the spirit of Judas, the spirit of Absalom & Jezebel spirit is very cunning.

You all remember Judas, false humility acting, Absalom, King David's son, who in return deceived the whole kingdom and even King David's right hand man to follow Absalom, his intentions of the heart were deceiving. You all have already studied the spirit of Jezebel that causes division any way she could in many different forms of characteristics. There is a lot of psychologically doctrine that's been preached into your spirits, most people accept the tolerance because your lonely, insecure in some areas of your life and dreadfully need attention any way you can get it. You want to be used by God, which is wonderful and can be understood, but the aspect of it all you must wait and come to understanding of Spiritual timing, you need discipline or discipleship from the Holy spirit. Say this really loud a revelation that was given to me 6 years ago on my knees the Holy spirit spoke softly, Curse Rebellion off of you!. Yes you can curse rebellion off of you. In the Book of Acts they went to the upper room and waited until the power of God fell upon them and inside them.

You need to wait have patience, but most assuredly its very difficult for you to separate yourselves from ungodly soul ties and possibly your just bored of your life. The spirit of ignorance stubbornness and rebellion is very strong within you.

Everyone's walk of life calling & commission and seasons is different from other Saints, just because you all go to the same church you do everything they profess or ask of you. A main prophet in the body of Christ a Prophet stated which was so true, if your ministry does not except that you have gifts and talents and does not allow you to utilize them, run out of the building and never return. Of course the leadership needs to ask the Holy spirit if they need deliverance or healing in any kind of way. Above all the Father looks at our attitude, we need to a good attitude towards everyone and not have a critical spirit. You all know what critical means, do you lash out at people very easy, always murmuring complaining, causing mischief amongst others. Critical spirit, having character assassinating talk or speeches or have ill will toward someone.

Here is a reference in the inclusion statement about an Apostle asking Yeshua about someone's own walk of life and Yeshua's words John 21 verse 21When Peter saw him, he said to Jesus, Lord, what about this man?

22 Jesus said to him, If I want him to stay (survive, live) until I come, what is that to you? [What concern is it of yours?] You follow Me!

23 So word went out among the brethren that this disciple was not going to die; yet Jesus did not say to him that he was not going to die, but, If I want him to stay (survive, live) till I come, what is that

to you? Yeshua's words mind your own business (beeswax) what or how I deal with others when it comes to favor, mercy, grace etc. Yeshua has specifically spoke to others giving them such an abundance of favor and grace and mercy, telling them you do not have to fast anymore, My son does not have to work!. Now your own insecurity issues and logic drives you insane, its called jealously & envy or ill will toward someone. Yes my beloved children your hate and suffering of pain within your heart drives you mad cause your not treated so graciously. God is not the problem its you, Yes my beloved children a young man was attacked on all sides. One Prophet called in his spiritual mother from Los Angeles California, cause he couldn't figure out this young maturing prophets life, The prophet came in and rebuked the leaders and said God Yahweh told me this young man is not to work with his bare hands. The Holy spirit spoke specifically in detail if you come against this, your committing treason against God himself.

This young man was astonished and felt better concerning himself even though he was still living in such distress and hardships. Check this out 6months later another Prophetess was on a 21 day fast and she knows the mother of this child and she called the mother and gave her what the father spoke to her about. She stated to the mother I don't know how your gonna take this but the Father said your son is not supposed to work he has Wealth beyond his understanding and the father is bringing it to him by his hands. The mother laughed cause she knew within her spirit her son was telling the truth. But some of us love to use our two cent opinions about everyone else except asking the Holy spirit. When it goes against the doctrine you have been taught or impregnated with it shakes you or you convulse spiritually. Her are some other references for transformation, be careful these books are very detailed and hits you hard where its needed. The first one The Hebrew Prophets by Rabbi Rami Shapiro, Second 12 steps to the Recovering Pharisee (like me) by John Fischer, third Tortured for Christ by Richard Wurmbrand, 4th Charles Swindoll Improve your serve. These books will cut you deep and penetrate you for transformation, if your ready for truth and Holy Spirit fire then by all means prepare for your Destiny Call & Commission. When most of the people I informed about these books and actually given them to read they returned the books to me within 2 days or 2 weeks and did not comment, all they stated I'm not ready to read something like that. They read the first chapter and shut it, closed it and returned the books back to me. Here are some instructions of being bold like manner in ministry, when a speaker just because they can prophesy and they begin to shove people to the floor by their own flesh and its not the Holy Spirit making them go down or backward, you say to them If they call you out, Do not lay hands on me or shove me to the floor please and be abrupt about it. Don't be scared to speak to the so called leader speaking, when you go into a meeting or service, speak and declare Dominion, Authority and the spirit of truth in this house, I want to be under Gods tent and not mans. Cover yourself speak these words Let not my soul enter in their council nor let my glory unite in their wicked assembly. Genesis 49:6, O my soul, come not into their secret council; unto their assembly let not my honor be united [for I knew nothing of their plot], because in their anger they slew men [an honored man, Shechem, and the Shechemites], and in their self-will they disabled oxen.

Yes my beloved Saints & children when there is a (Tent of meetings) both spiritual forces are there, All the host of heaven and the Demonic host of Hell! Discerning of spirits, test the spirits, do not believe every spirit, this teaching needs to be administered more than ever. Here my beloved Saints get ready to dive into the Holy of Holies of Understanding!. Let me give you a Revelation concerning the book of Matthew 25: 33-36 When I was hungry you didn't feed me, When I was in prison you didn't come visit me, when I was naked you didn't clothe me. When I was naked of the Christ within you, us ourselves you didn't clothe me with his character, understanding of who he is, clothing in Hebrew mean (Character functions) Revelation 3:17 For you say, I am rich; I have prospered *and* grown wealthy, and I am in need of nothing; and you do not realize *and* understand that you are wretched, pitiable, poor, blind, and naked. When I was hungry you didn't feed me, we didn't feed ourselves with his word the three levels of eating, milk, bread & meat. When I was in prison you didn't come visit me, Saints we ourselves have kept Yeshua in prison within ourselves. When I was thirsty you didn't give me a drink, Matthew 10 41:42, If you give a Prophet a revelation he will pour out back to the children & Saints of God his rewards from heaven the Father Yahweh.

John 2 1-12,verse 7 Jesus said to them, Fill the water pots with water. So they filled them up to the brim.8 Then He said to them, Draw some out now and take it to the manager of the feast [to the one presiding, the superintendent of the banquet]. So they took him some. 9 And when the manager tasted the water just now turned into wine, not knowing where it came from—though the servants who had drawn the water knew—he called the bridegroom. Master of the feast which is the father, Yeshua saying take this new wine and take this knew revelation and let Dad the father taste it to confirm it. But the servants the prophets know where the new wine, the rain of revelation is coming from & how its being poured forth to fulfill the plan of Yahweh. Only the servants the prophets knew where it was coming from.

Amos chap 3 7 Surely the Lord God will do nothing [a]without revealing His secret to His servants the prophets. Revelation transforms our minds, secrets of the kingdom, that's the rapture he speaks of new information. New Revelation understanding of the correct interpretation not dry no Holy spirit false religious doctrine. Genesis 3:24 24 So [God] drove out the man; and He placed at the east of the Garden of Eden the [c]cherubim and a flaming sword which turned every way, to keep *and* guard the way to the tree of life. The flaming sword was the Fire of Yahweh the secret mysteries and veld understandings,. The fire of Yahweh came down, they were baptized through their minds, burning all their carnal understandings, reasoning's & logic. All the apostles denied Christ at one point, until the book of Acts. The book of Acts 2, particularly verse 28 You have made known to me the ways of life; You will enrapture me [diffusing my soul with joy] with *and* in Your presence. En-rapture (to move to rapture; delight beyond measure:). Diffuse- to pour out and spread, as a fluid. All religious false doctrine that we were impregnated with across all nations, we are being baptized to burn it all out.

Here this saints Luke 17:8 Will he not instead tell him, Get my supper ready and gird yourself and serve me while I eat and drink; then afterward you yourself shall eat and drink? Gird thyself prepare for me, serve me within you (for we are the temple of the Holy Spirit & we do not belong to ourselves this body is his), while I eat & drink the Yeshua within us to prepare us for his Service for the Kingdom. We are entering in the Wedding feast here & now to become one with him just like Elijah, to walk how Yeshua walked!.

Milk of the word, baby in Christ immaturity, Bread the discipleship, training, molding brokenness, eat of my body for it was broken for us, **Colossians 2:8** - Beware lest any man spoil you through philosophy and vain deceit, after the tradition of men, after the rudiments of the world, and not after Christ. What kind of food are you being feed with, Meat refining of Purified fire, revelation mysteries of the kingdom. Malachi 3:3 He will sit as a refiner and purifier of silver, and He will purify the priests, the sons of Levi, and refine them like gold and silver, that they may offer to the Lord offerings in righteousness.

The father speaks of The Prophets tongue, his motive & intentions of the Heart, the correct interpretation of his word through revelation, Malachi 2:7 For the priest's lips should guard *and* keep pure the knowledge [of My law], and the people should seek (inquire for and require) instruction at his mouth; for he is the messenger of the Lord of hosts. He also speaks to his children the Priests, for he calls us all a kingdom of priests. The Timing of the spirit is hear, 2 Timothy 4:3 For the time will come when people will not put up with sound doctrine. Instead, to suit their own desires, they will gather around them a great number of teachers to say what their itching ears want to hear. Tithe & offering saints has nothing to with money, bring thy tithe so that there may be meat in my house (The temple of the Holy Spirit which is us) As you allow me to Baptize you with Fire, meat revelation the correct understanding, refined in what kind of offerings, reverence to me whole heartedly, complete wholeness all your heart mind body soul and strength. I shall pour out a blessing you cant handle, I will rapture you with information of secrets, mysteries that you can pour back out to others.

Malachi 3:11 And I will rebuke the devourer [insects and plagues] for your sakes and he shall not destroy the fruits of your ground, neither shall your vine drop its fruit before the time in the field, says the Lord of hosts. I will prevent pests (witchcraft, human spirits, demoniac s, devouring your crops, your inheritance, the Favor Kingly Priestly anointing of Melchizedek). What is the vine, the Christ of Yahweh within us, the ministry of his outpouring, sending the messengers out to the fields. They will not cast there fruit, they will not deny Christ, it will not allow for your characteristics and personalities, your motive and intentions of your heart to be polluted with sound doctrine. You begin to deny Christ when your fruit of his character is polluted within you, when you receive religion, compromise, complacency, seered conscious (cauterized). 1 Corinthians 3:19 For the wisdom of this world is foolishness to God. As the Scriptures say, "He traps the wise in the snare of their own cleverness." Casting your fruits for private gain, prostituting one another. Just like Lucifer the angel on the Ark of the Covenant, casting his fruit, he had 12stones. He deceived a third of the angels. He cast his fruit to the ground, he only has 9stones now.

Matthew 7:15 Beware of false prophets, who come to you dressed as sheep, but inside they are devouring wolves.16 You will [l]fully recognize them by their fruits. Do people pick grapes from thorns, or figs from thistles? 17 Even so, every healthy (sound) tree bears good fruit [[m]worthy of admiration], but the sickly (decaying, worthless) tree bears bad (worthless) fruit. 18 A good (healthy) tree cannot bear bad (worthless) fruit, nor can a bad (diseased) tree bear [n]excellent fruit [worthy of admiration]. 19 Every tree that does not bear good fruit is cut down and cast into the fire.20 Therefore, you will [o]fully know them by their fruits.21 Not everyone who says to Me, Lord, Lord, will enter the kingdom of heaven, but he who does the will of My Father Who is in heaven.22 Many will say to Me on that day, Lord, Lord, have we not prophesied in Your name and driven out demons in Your name and done many mighty works in Your name?23 And then I will say to them openly (publicly), I never knew you; depart from Me, you who act wickedly [disregarding My commands]. There are workers in the Ministry who have already been casting their fruits in the field and denying Christ and have made covenants with evil foul spirits and don't even know it at all or even there in self denial about it.

Moses was prepared to walk into the Presence of God Yahweh, the burning bush. The father has allowed certain sons to walk, preach, prophecy, use the gifts & talents, do the work of ministry service, but saying they will never come unto me or come near me. A lot of false sound doctrine preachers Prognosticate this scripture and tie it to tithing. Matthew 5:17 Do not think that I have come to abolish the law or the prophets. I have not come to abolish them but to fulfill them. What he meant was I have come to give you the right correct interpretation of the word through revelation. Here and last but not least some specific instructions about loving one another that saints are afraid to speak up against the so called leaders, 2 Timothy 4:1-4 In the presence of God and of Christ Jesus, who will judge the living and the dead, and in view of his appearing and his kingdom, I give you this charge: 2 Preach the word; be prepared in season and out of season; correct, rebuke and encourage—with great patience and careful instruction. Yes its ok to correct one another, rebuke one another and after encourage- with great patience and careful instruction with unconditional love.

Ok Saints here is a scripture reference just in case you forgot, Matthew 7: New International Version.

"Do not give dogs what is sacred; do not throw your pearls to pigs. If you do, they may trample them under their feet, and turn and tear you to pieces. "Don't waste what is holy on people who are unholy. Don't throw your pearls to pigs! They will trample the pearls, then turn and attack you. Have you noticed that most of the of the attacks you receive is coming from religious saints, Christian friends or whatever religion is pronounced or proclaim there from. Here let me give you an illustration of a Jezebel spirit, one pastor in the city of San Jacinto California, did not know even know he had two of them in his ministry. I sat about ten rows in the back of his own house where the ministry was but it was a huge house. This one young lad came up to me and handed me a flier from the ministry, I told him thank you but its OK, because I knew I was there just as a guest. His eyes and his whole physiology went cockeyed for a few seconds, now his mother which had the Jezebel spirit, was ten rows in the front, had no clue what was going on in the back, especially ten rows back. She immediately stood up and walked tens rows back, then grabbed the flier from her sons hand and then tried to offer it again to me, I said no thanks. His mother which Jezebel spirits do they control your emotions and feelings, and they even transfer there souls within you for control. I looked at the young lad and even his emotions would change within seconds several times. The Holy Spirit revealed to me that was a Jezebel spirit controlling her sons emotions and feelings and even his posture and physiology. The Holy Spirit revealed to me, the spirit of Jezebel transfers there souls into their victims like a false anointing spirit. Its a false peace that comes along with it.

ANTHONY MONTOYA

ABOUT THE AUTHOR

Hello family, I am just going to give you a brief illustration of my Testimony about my life In Yahshua. I'm currently divorced over 10 years one daughter, my daughter is 13 one of the greatest life's experiences in my life. My parents are Ministers of the good news for the last 45years experience in the prophetic call and commission. My father's an Apostle and my mother's a Prophetess, who's been used for 17 years. I've been trained under the Holy Spirit and will always be in training, ever since my walk I've been taught to die to self and to lay down my own self will for the sake of the Kingdom for transformation. My biological father left me when I was 11, I had an encounter with God himself, the Father when I was 18 years of age.

One day everyone was gone, my mother had three children I am the middle child, it was around midnight walking around my home. I spoke to myself and stated I was all alone then the phone rang it was weird, then I said hello the voice said" Are you alone" I then said who is this. The voice continued and said "This is your Father, your not alone." Then I said, "ok who is this, stop playing around!" The voice continued and said, "Go to the mirror and then stated are you alone?" Then I said, "Who is this the voice?" Then he continued, "This is your Father in Heaven." I was stunned for that moment and couldn't grasp or understand the situation and my brain went blank.

Since that day, I've been divorced ten years, slept in the streets homeless for about 6 years, kicked out of churches for being too prophetic, slept in houses with ministers who are apostles and prophets that astro projected out of their bodies.

While I have disobeyed Yahweh several times, he allowed me to see the demonic realm and was attacked heavily by my own disobedience, also by other leaders that have mastered the gift inside them using for their own self gain. Trained under the gift of the discerning of spirits, to discern the motive and intents of the hearts of the people around me.

I was just recently pulled out from being homeless, several years ago about 2 ½ to be precise, generational curses broken off from biological father who made a deal with Satan, An apostle prophesied and stated your biological father made a deal with Satan to have the blood of two of his children for promise for money for the rest of his life. My sister was cured from whooping cough there was no cure at that time. I was set free from several demonic spirits that are so real. My walk in ministry was to discern why so much division, only by Yahshua's grace and the Holy Spirit has graced me to understand the spirit of influence & religion using venom of false doctrine and false prophecies that's been impregnated in the hearts of gods children & have been left crippled and shuts down their own immune system.

My present state I'm ordained minister, my belief is to be a life living sacrifice for Yahweh's kingdom, only to be servant to others and help one another reach Yahweh's purpose and destiny in our lives. To unveil the mysteries and revelations of this kingdom age for all his children to be set free from religion, jezebel spirits, spirit of influence, psychology, false hope (false prophesies), rejection, abandonment guilt, shame, control, seared conscious, subconscious, conscious, mesocratic cells, trauma, familiar spirits, camellia spirits that transforms and changes color, cockatrice spirit, the false god of Prosperity, Fortune & Destiny, mystical influences that general spirits have had dominion over us.

Isaiah [13] O Lord, our God, other masters besides You have ruled over us, but we will acknowledge *and* mention Your name only.[14] They [the former tyrant masters] are dead, they shall not live *and* reappear; they are powerless ghosts, they shall not rise *and* come back. Therefore You have visited and made an end of them and caused every memory of them [every trace of their supremacy] to perish. This reference speaks of general demonic spirits even with all religious practices, he will even wipe away the memory of them out of us.

MINISTRY CONTACT INFORMATION

You may contact Anthony Montoya

through the following sources:

Email Address:

Judah1231@yahoo.com

Website:

anthonymontoyas1.weebly.com

www.ingramcontent.com/pod-product-compliance
Lightning Source LLC
Chambersburg PA
CBHW062018040426
42447CB00010B/2046